Feeling ove[r]
by challeng[...]

CW01583878

Some of the common reasons for feeling stressed or low is because of the problems we face in life. Sometimes these problems are very large - things like losing a job, having to move house, or a relationship breakdown.

However, small problems can also be overwhelming when they build up. Each individual thing might be something we can tackle quite easily, but when they keep coming one after another they can slowly grind us down.

This little book teaches ways of tackling problems. It works particularly well if you're feeling low or stressed, and so overwhelmed by problems you don't know where to start. It doesn't matter what you want to work on, our plan can help*.

The idea is to break your problem or goal into manageable chunks that, by themselves, are easier to do.

Often you may be facing many problems at the same time. Choose a single problem you want to work on that will make a difference to how you feel. **Write it here:**

____

Now discover our Easy 4-Step Plan

*Well - it can't make the sun shine if it's raining - but you could plan to take an umbrella.

STEP 1

BREAK IT INTO CHUNKS

Solving a problem is like climbing a wall

It may look far too big to deal with. But when you break it into smaller bits it's less scary and easier to manage.

That's why Step 1 of our **Easy 4 Step Plan** (E4SP) is 'break it into chunks'.

Perhaps you feel you never see your friends. You could break the week into chunks and make an effort to see them on Mondays, for example.

If you think you are spending too much time alone you could try watching TV with someone a couple of nights a week instead of sitting in your room.

Or if you feel you're on social media or watching TV too much, you could start by not doing it for an afternoon or a day.

Most problems can be chopped up like this, and you're much more likely to succeed when you do things bit by bit.

Turn over for **STEP 2**

STEP 2

THINK OF CREATIVE WAYS TO TACKLE THE FIRST CHUNK

Feeling stuck for a solution?

When we feel stressed it often feels harder to find solutions. This is when it can help to be creative and let your mind run free. Think of as many solutions as possible, whether they are realistic or silly, to help your ideas flow. Why not note them down on your phone, or a piece of paper.

For example:

1. If you want to get out more often, you could go for a walk, or find a new hobby to do outside like gardening? Or perhaps start training together for the local marathon which takes place next week having never run before?*

2. Spending too much time watching TV? Get in touch with a friend and have a catch up. Why not play a board game? Or turn the TV off while you are eating and chat about your day or plans you have for the future? Or take the TV to your local tip?*

3. Want to cut down the time you spend on social media or playing games on your phone? Leave your phone in another room, forget your phone on purpose one day when you go out? Perhaps block social media sites, or set a time limit for using them? Maybe put it on silent or turn it off at a set time each day? Plan something fun or engaging to do instead? Or give your phone away?*

STEP 3 next

* In being creative we have included some unrealistic or even silly ideas.

STEP 3

CHOOSE AN IDEA AND MAKE A PLAN TO DO IT

Look at your list of creative ideas and pick one

Choose one that seems realistic and achievable. Now write down, step by step **how** and **when** to actually DO it. Make the chunks as small as you like, but not so small you don't make any progress.

1. So, if you want to get out more often make a plan of the day and time to do this. Plan when you'll get up. Get dressed, leave the house and walk to the local shops.

2. Spending too much time watching TV? Text a friend suggesting the day and time you meet up and decide what you will do. Again agree a time and place for your catch up.

3. Want to cut down the time you spend on social media or playing games on your phone? Choose a time to spend with your family or friends doing something that you enjoy. What will you plan - and when?

What if something gets in the way?

As soon as you've written your plan, think about what could stop it happening. Is there anything that might trip you up? What about the reactions of other people? Could someone be unhelpful at any stage? Or might you feel tired or demotivated? Or perhaps you talk yourself out of it?

When you've figured out what might block your progress, work out a mini-plan for getting round the obstacle.

This way, you'll be ready for whatever happens!

Final step coming up

STEP 4

CHECK THE PLAN AND PUT IT INTO ACTION

This is it! You've written down all the steps, now use this checklist:

Is it realistic? ☐

You're not planning to run a marathon are you?

Are you aiming at just one thing? ☐

You can always pick another when you've sorted the first one.

Is it slow? ☐

There's no need to rush at things. Your plan can take as long as you like, so long as you stick to it, step by step.

Is it easy? ☐

Make your steps small and easy and you'll be more likely to do them. But not so small you see no difference.

Are you ready to unblock it? ☐

Have you thought about what could go wrong and how to deal with it?

✓✓✓✓✓

FIVE TICKS?

Then Go for it!

living
life to
the full
www.llttf.com

Easy 4-Step Plan

My problem

Before you start: If you're facing lots of challenges - pick just one to work on first. Write it here:

Will changing it have a helpful impact on how you feel, or on your situation? ☐

1 Break it into chunks

List the different ideas you could take to move things forward:

What would get you on your way? Not too large so it's unrealistic- or too small so that it doesn't address the problem.

Choose the first thing/chunk you will work on:

2 Think of creative ways to tackle the first chunk*

(*include creative and silly ideas as well as more sensible ones)

From the:
Living life to the full
resources.

Download from
www.llttf.com

3 Choose an idea and make a plan to do it

Write your idea here:

Create a plan to do it and write it here:

When are you going to do it?
(that way you will know if you don't do it):

Write down any **problems or difficulties** that could arise - and how you can overcome them:

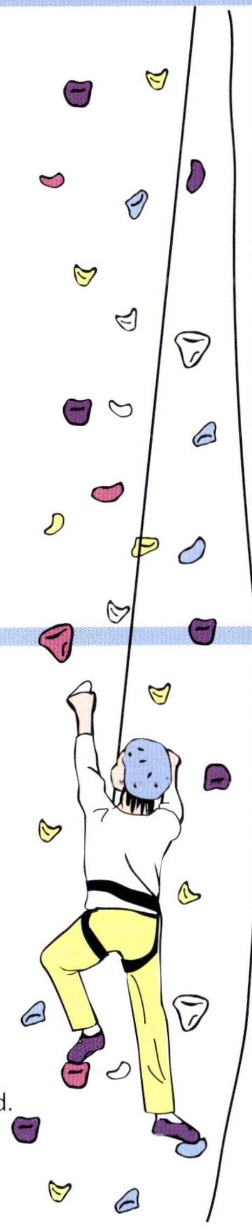

4 Check the plan and put it into action

- [ ] Are you aiming at just one thing?
- [ ] Is it realistic?
- [ ] Is it slow?
- [ ] Is it easy?
- [ ] Are you ready to unblock it?

Once you've done (or not done) your plan - Review what happened.
What next? Continue your current plan or start something new?
Write it here:

NOW TRY OUT YOUR PLAN

Moving forward step by step

Now you have used the Easy 4-Step Plan to plan the first chunk, it's time to put it into action. Sounds easy? But we all know sometimes we can get stuck. Maybe we lose motivation? Or talk ourselves out of it, or maybe things change and the initial plan needs updating?

One of the most common reasons for not doing things is we forget. To help you stay on track, add the **time and day** you are going to carry out the first step of your plan into your phone or wall calendar. Or set a reminder using Alexa or Google home or similar.

You could also ask others to prompt, encourage or remind you. Sometimes just telling someone else what you plan to do can be a big help.

Keep working on your problem chunk by chunk using the **Easy 4-Step Plan worksheet**. If something is a larger or complicated problem, you will need to make a series of plans for each step/ chunk using the E4SP sheet.

Then use the **Review sheet** on the following pages to look at what has happened. What have you learned? How can you put what you've learned into practice as you make future plans?

LLTTF®
living
life to
the full
www.llttf.com

Review Sheet

How did it go?

What did you plan to do?

Did you try to do it? Yes ☐ No ☐

If yes: What went well?

What didn't go so well?

What have you learned from what happened?

How are you going to apply what you have learned?

If no: What stopped you?

You: (forgot, not enough time, put it off, didn't think I could do it, couldn't see the point etc.)

Other things: (other people, work or home issues, poor weather, transport difficulties etc.)

How can you tackle things differently next time?

WHAT TO DO WHEN THE GOING GETS TOUGH

Try these ideas to remind you why you started in the first place

- Remind yourself why you want to make the change. Write it down and put it where you can see it.
- How will things be in 2-3 weeks/months/ years if you don't make the changes?
- Note down the benefits of changing for you, or others. Perhaps better health, sorting out the leaking roof, better relationships, keeping a job, having more friends, having more fun, having more money, doing better overall?
- Tell as many people as possible what you're doing, so that they can help you (or encourage you if you slip).

Ready for some real-life examples?

If you're not sure how to apply the plan to your problem, the next few pages will help. They're full of real plans showing how people like you have fixed different things and turned their lives around.

How the **Easy 4-Step Plan** works in real life

LLTTF® living life to the full www.llttf.com

Easy 4-Step Plan Example 1

My problem

Before you start: If you're facing lots of challenges - pick just one to work on first. Write it here:

I want to make new friends

Will changing it have a helpful impact on how you feel, or on your situation? ✓

1 Break it into chunks

List the different ideas you could take to move things forward:

List the people I know already that I'd like to get to know better.

List the people who I haven't spoken to or met/hung out with for a while.

Stop eating alone in the canteen and sit with other people.

Ask people I know to introduce me to other people.

Join a club or society. If it involves sports or fitness, I could crack two problems at once!

Pay an actor to pretend to be my friend (that's the silly idea!)

What would get you on your way? Not too large so it's unrealistic- or too small so that it doesn't address the problem.

Choose the first thing/chunk you will work on: *List the people I already know that I'd like get to know better.*

2 Think of creative ways to tackle the first chunk*

Look up the contact details of old friends. Make a list of the people who I know but aren't in regular contact with. Also those who I added on Instagram or swapped numbers with but have never contacted.

If I have no way of contacting them but I know their name, add them on Instagram or Facebook with a friendly message. Now take a look at those whose numbers I have, and those who are already my social media friends.

(*include creative and silly ideas as well as more sensible ones)

3 Choose an idea and make a plan to do it

Write your idea here: List the people I know already that I'd like to get to know better

Create a plan to do it and write it here:

Look through my phone and look at my contacts. Look up people I know from school/college/university/work/my street who I haven't seen for ages.

When are you going to do it?
(that way you will know if you don't do it): This evening after eating (8pm)

Write down any **problems or difficulties** that could arise - and how you can overcome them:

- I might forget - so I'll set a reminder on my phone.
- They may not answer in which case I could just move on to the next person in the list.

4 Check the plan and put it into action

- [x] Are you aiming at just one thing?
- [x] Is it realistic?
- [x] Is it slow?
- [x] Is it easy?
- [x] Are you ready to unblock it?

Once you've done (or not done) your plan - Review what happened.
What next? Continue your current plan - or start something new?
Write it here: Sit with other people in the canteen at lunchtime

living life to the full
www.llttf.com

Review Sheet
Example 1

How did it go? **What did you plan to do?**

List the people I know already that I'd like get to know better.

Did you try to do it? Yes ✓ No ☐

If yes: **What went well?**

I got a list of 7–8 people I'd like to catch up with

What didn't go so well?

I didn't save the list of names to start with and lost it on my phone. I had to start again.

What have you learned from what happened?

Save the list or write it down on a piece of paper.

From the:
Living life to the full
resources.

Download from www.llttf.com

How are you going to apply what you have learned?

Writing it down on a piece of paper works better for me for this sort of thing

If no: What stopped you?

You: (forgot, not enough time, put it off, didn't think I could do it, couldn't see the point etc.)

Other things: (other people, work or home issues, poor weather, transport difficulties etc.)

How can you tackle things differently next time?

WHAT WOULD BE THE NEXT STEP?

After the first step - what happens next?

Creating a list of people who you already know and you would like to get to know better only addresses the first chunk/part of the problem.

After doing this, there are a series of additional steps.

For example:

- Choose one person from the list and text or call them up. Or send them a message on Facebook or Instagram.
- In the message say *"Hi - I haven't seen you for ages"*. Then invite them to go for a coffee or walk.
- If they are someone you know from work or college, why not ask them a question about a difficult piece of work as a conversation opener?

You can repeat this process with the next person on the list until someone replies and you meet up. Be kind to yourself if it doesn't work immediately.

You can complete a series of E4SP worksheets to plan further steps that build on this first one. If you get stuck you can always revisit the list of chunks that address your problem in Step 1 of the E4SP worksheet (page 20) and try another one.

LLTTF® living life to the full www.llttf.com

Easy 4-Step Plan Example 2

My problem

Before you start: If you're facing lots of challenges - pick just one to work on first. Write it here:

I need to revise for my history exam

Will changing it have a helpful impact on how you feel, or on your situation? ✓

1 Break it into chunks

List the different ideas you could take to move things forward:

Make a timetable so that I cover everything in time for the exam.

Find a friend who's doing the same exam and work together.

Divide the week into revision periods and don't go out/watch TV at those times.

Decide on three days a week for revision and turn my phone off or leave it with someone else at those times.

Pitch a tent in the garden so I can do all their revision in there, away from the TV.

Go to the library and get some books out about revision technique.

Go and stay with a relative who only has a black and white TV. (that's the silly one!)

What would get you on your way? Not too large so it's unrealistic- or too small so that it doesn't address the problem.

Choose the first thing/chunk you will work on: *Make a timetable so I cover everything in time for the exam*

2 Think of creative ways to tackle the first chunk*

Find the date of the exam
Find the syllabus from the exam board website
Create a list of topics to study
Check class notes and text books for topics to cover
Decide just 10 minutes a week will help me remember the key stuff (that's the silly one)

(*include creative and silly ideas as well as more sensible ones)

3 Choose an idea and make a plan to do it

Write your idea here: *Create a list of topics to study*

Create a plan to do it and write it here:

Find the exam date online.

List the topics we've covered in class.

Speak to my history teacher about which topics are likely to come up.

From all this create a list of the topics I'm going to cover.

When are you going to do it?
(that way you will know if you don't do it) *My deadline is to do this before the end of the week*

What **problems or difficulties** could arise
- and how can you overcome them?

It might be hard to speak to my history teacher. To tackle this I could email them.
The exam board website might be complicated. If so I could ask a friend to help.

4 Check the plan and put it into action

- [x] Are you aiming at just one thing?
- [x] Is it realistic?
- [x] Is it slow?
- [x] Is it easy?
- [x] Are you ready to unblock it?

Once you've done (or not done) your plan - Review what happened.
What next? Continue your current plan - or start something new?
Write it here: *Add the list of topics to my calendar. Choose a date/time to cover the topics I will study*

LLTTF® living life to the full www.llttf.com

Review Sheet
Example 2

How did it go? What did you plan to do?

Create a list of topics to study before the end of the week

Did you try to do it? Yes ☐ No ☑

If yes: What went well?

What didn't go so well?

What have you learned from what happened?

From the:
Living life to the full
resources.

How are you going to apply what you have learned?

If no: What stopped you?

You: (forgot, not enough time, put it off, didn't think I could do it, couldn't see the point etc.)

On the first evening I'd had a tough day and got home feeling tired. I decided to put it off to the next day.

Other things: (other people, work or home issues, poor weather, transport difficulties etc.)

The next day the wifi wasn't working at home and I had a poor phone signal so I couldn't get online.
The history teacher was off sick.

How can you tackle things differently next time?

1. Even if I feel tired I can do a bit of work. If I'd done that when the wifi was working it would really have helped.
2. I sent the teacher an email so they'll respond when they can.

WHAT IF YOU GET STUCK?

Don't worry, you can do it

The Easy 4-Step Plan (E4SP) works, even when you have a really tough problem to deal with.

Remember the climbing wall - you can get to the top step by step. All you have to do is keep on climbing!

To help you with this use the Easy 4-Step Plan worksheet.

PASS ON WHAT YOU'VE LEARNED

Discovered something good?

If so, that's great! Why not share what you've learned with someone else who might benefit?

- A son or daughter?
- A partner?
- A friend or other relative?
- Someone you work with?

Most people face times when they feel stuck, pressured or overwhelmed. The E4SP can be a helpful solution for them when they feel like this.

So, once you've mastered this approach, why not pass it on! You may also discover that helping others is a great way of also helping yourself feel a sense of pleasure and achievement.

Go for it!

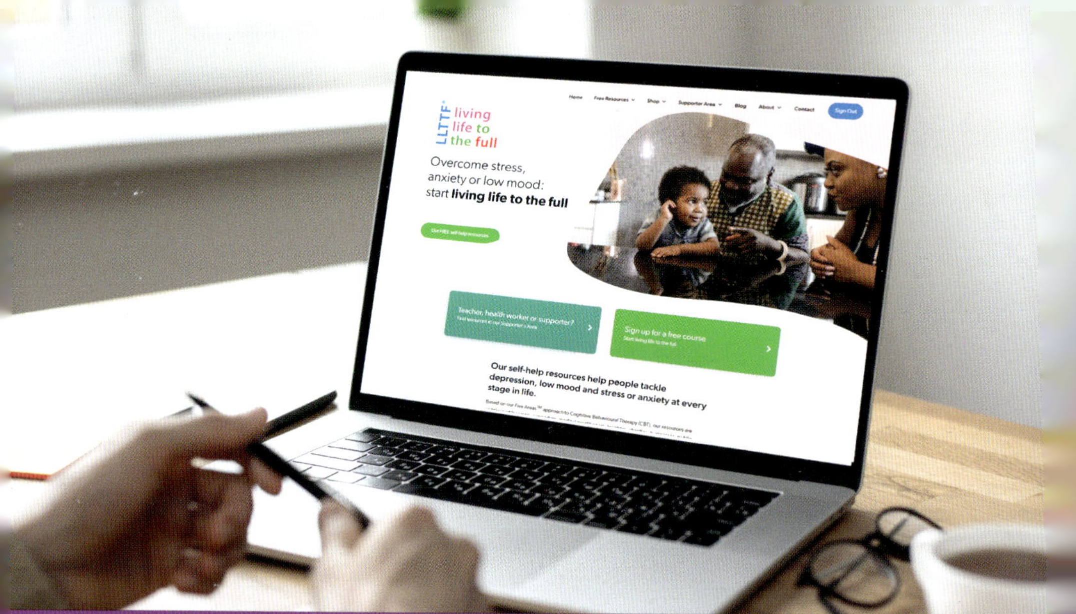

NOW IT'S YOUR TURN!

As the real life examples show, the Easy 4-Step Plan works really well. All you have to do is take it step by step and be steady and determined.

You can get added advice and support on this approach by working through the free linked courses at www.llttf.com. When you've sorted out your current problems, you might want to choose another topic and work on something else in your life.